Animals on the farm

Sue Barraclough

Heinemann
LIBRARY

Little Nippers

www.heinemann.co.uk/library
Visit our website to find out more information about **Heinemann Library** books.

To order:
☎ Phone 44 (0) 1865 888066
▤ Send a fax to 44 (0) 1865 314091
▥ Visit the Heinemann Bookshop at www.heinemann.co.uk/library to browse our
catalogue and order online.

First published in Great Britain by
Heinemann Library, Halley Court, Jordan Hill,
Oxford OX2 8EJ, part of Harcourt Education.
Heinemann is a registered trademark of Harcourt
Education Ltd.

Editorial: Sarah Shannon and Dave Harris
Design: Jo Hinton-Malivoire and bigtop design ltd
Picture Research: Ruth Blair and Kay Altwegg
Production: Chloe Bloom

Originated by Modern Age
Printed and bound in China by South China
Printing Company

ISBN 0 431 00363 7 (hardback)
10 09 08 07 06
10 9 8 7 6 5 4 3 2 1

ISBN 0 431 00368 8 (paperback)
10 09 08 07 06
10 9 8 7 6 5 4 3 2 1

British Library Cataloguing in Publication Data
Barraclough, Sue
    Animals on the farm. - (Animal worlds)
    636
A full catalogue record for this book is available
from the British Library.

Acknowledgements
The publishers would like to thank the following
for permission to reproduce photographs:
Agripicture p. 11; Agripicture/Peter Dean pp. 10,
16, 19, 20, 21; Alamy/D Hurst p. 22;
Alamy/Robert Harding Picture Library Ltd p. 13;
Ardea/Jean Michel Labat p. 14; Bruce Coleman
pp. 16, 17; Corbis p. 6; Corbis/Ariel Skelley pp. 4,
5; Corbis/Philip Gould p. 23; FLPA/Gerard Lacz p.
7; FLPA/Heidi Hans-Juergen Koch; Minden
Pictures p. 18; FLPA/Sunset p. 12; Harcourt Index
p. 9; Naturepl.com/Lynn M Stone p. 8; NHPA/ p.
15; NHPA/Susanne Danegger pp. 17, 19.

Cover photograph reproduced with permission
of photolibrary.com/osf.

Contents

Have you ever been to a farm?

Cows, sheep, and goats live on farms.

Different farm animals

Chickens are farm animals too.

Chickens have feathers all over their bodies.

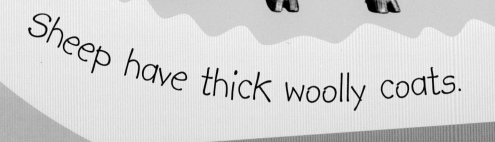

Sheep have thick woolly coats.

What is your favourite farm animal?

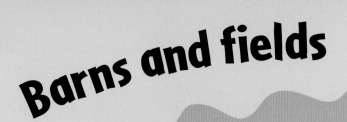

Farm animals live in fields and barns.

These cows have plenty of green grass to munch.

8

Chickens are kept in a house at night to keep them safe.

The farmer lets them out in the morning.

9

Food and water

Farm animals need to eat food.

Peck!

Peck!

These chicks eat grain from a dish.

Farm animals need water to drink, too.

Slurp!

This cow takes a long drink.

Useful animals

Farm animals give us food such as cheese and milk.

Can you think of which animal gives us eggs?

Sheep have their woolly coats cut off in the summer.

We can make warm clothes with the wool.

13

Baby farm animals

Baby farm animals have special names.

Baby pigs are called piglets. Baby sheep are called lambs.

Moving around

Geese **waddle** from side to side as they walk.

Young lambs **leap** when they play.

Horses move *fast* when they run.

Making noises

Farm animals make all kinds of noises.

Cock-a-doodle-doo!

Can you make these animal noises?

Baaa!

What is your favourite farm animal sound?

Moo!

Calling the vet

Animals have special doctors, called vets.

If a farm animal is sick, the vet comes out to the farm.

This vet gives an animal medicine to make it better.

Caring and cleaning

There is plenty of work to do on a farm.